Parent's Guide to IEPs

Dr. Sophia Latrell Crawford- Mapp

PARENT'S GUIDE TO IEPS

A guide to navigate Special Education/ Exceptional Children's Program

Dr. Sophia Crawford- Mapp

Sophia Latrell Publishing

Sophia Latrell
Publishing

Copyright 2020 Dr. Sophia Crawford-Mapp

All rights reserved

ISBN

978-1-7349679-3-7

Printed in the United States of America

Table of content

Introductions

The thought of an Individual Education Plan (IEP) can be a big pill to swallow for several reasons: noticing your child needs more support than most, people using acronyms instead of words, navigating a legal document, etc. It is a big task and I am an educator. I don't take it lightly when I bring the subject up with a parent or student and I don't take it lightly when a parent or students asks me about it. Determining that a child needs this level of support is a HUGE notion or it should be.

I have been supporting students with IEPs my entire education career. It can be a great benefit for a 3-year-old entering school on their birthday and receiving support that can change their lives or a middle school student being identified before they head off to high school the biggest educational beast of them all.

It is my intention to give you as parents an understanding of the major concepts and points when navigating the special education or exceptional children's world. It may have either name, but the concepts are the same regardless of age, grade or state.

I am going to start this book with the step that is often neglected but I feel is the most important of them all and that is pinpointing exactly what your child needs and strengths are. This is vital because it will shape the first step to support your child effectively and efficiently. This happens in the problem-solving phase. It can also be called response to intervention (RTI), multi-tier support system (MTSS) or just intervention. Regardless of the name this is something to keep your thumb on and to ask lots of questions.

Identifying the strengths and needs

The key to supporting your child during their educational journey is to know what they are good at and what they need to work on. I believe the key to this is being specific and hammering it down to the smallest and lowest level. I want you to know this is not a minor task that is super simple. Within EVERY subject there is something that a child does well and something that they need to work on. The strengths and needs in one area can directly and indirectly impact other subjects. Let's just jump in and get specific, I am going to start with early childhood examples and work my way up to middle school.

As a parent you are your child's first teacher and you are Great at it! Yes, all of the parenting and child rearing books will say don't compare kids, but I am going to disagree with this a little. I am saying take the milestones that you know to be true and use them to make informed decisions about your child. No all children are not going to walk before they turn one year old but if your child isn't crawling by then a warning light should come on in your mind. All kids don't speak in short phrases by 2 but if your child has no interest or hasn't started to crudely communicate with you there should be a warning light on. The first person you should talk to about this is your child's pediatrician. If they say don't worry about it, you can let it go but if your warning lights are still on ASK someone else. Yes, this means you will have to see a different doctor but when it comes to your child it is your job to support and advocate for them.

Let's move up a few years and talk preschool. When your child enters preschool (public or private) there is an assessment that is going to be done. This assessment will review the five major domains: academics, speech and language, motor, self-help and socialization. Depending on the assessment, what is considered average is going to vary and this is okay. Regardless of what score is considered average, this will identify where your child is performing. There will be an overall score and a score for each level it is important that you ask where your child falls in each area because this will identify things that they can do well (strengths) and things they need to work on (needs). For example, your child could be deemed as average based on the entire assessment but the scores in each area doesn't mean that they are necessarily average in all areas. Your child could be above average in motor and below average in speech and language. This is why you need to ask for details. Average does not mean there isn't something to work on or does above average.

Here are a few things that each of the five major preschool assessments evaluate. Academics look at letters, numbers, book handling skills, etc. Speech and language look at how many words your child can speak, can they say all sounds, can they repeat longer phrases, etc. Motor skills look at how your child holds a pencil or a fork, how they walk, how they sit and stand, etc. Self-help notes if your child can feed and dress themselves, can they toilet and wash themselves, do they know rules, and more. Socialization evaluates if they play alone, beside or with kids, do they engage in make believe play and other group activities.

Elementary school is definitely when children are sorted and identified by ability level. Elementary school is typically when all subjects are taught and a student's ability level in all areas is known. This is when students are tested in either second or third grade to determine if they qualify for the gifted and talented (GT) or academically/intellectually gifted (AIG) programs or subjects. This is also when students start to take standardized local and state assessments.

Schools also start to give whole grade level benchmark assessments, and these are either school, district or state mandated. I am going to give a few examples such as Istation (state), NWEA MAP or Iready (district or school), or subject benchmarks (school, local or state). All of these assessments provide you with broad generalized scores such as one for reading and math and they also provide you with subareas for reading and subareas for math. On the NWEA MAP assessment, math can be broken down to statistics and probability, geometry, operations and algebraic thinking and real and complex number systems. It is one thing to say your child has a strength in math but it is something totally different to be specific to say your child is above average in statistics and probability, below average in geometry, average in operations and algebraic thinking and significantly below grade level in real and complex number systems. When you are having a conversation with the teacher about what to work on the latter information about specific sub-areas is more beneficial to a parent and teacher and student because it allows you to narrow your focus.

The same concepts apply to reading. I am going to shift assessments to speak about Iready to give another example but NWEA MAP has similar sub-areas. On the Iready assessment a student has an overall reading score as well as a score in phonological awareness, phonics, high frequency words, vocabulary, literature comprehension and informational text comprehension. Similar to math, it says more to talk areas of need by sub-areas than overall reading.

This will also apply to writing, social studies and science benchmark. A teacher would need to identify the sub- areas or standards that make up each subject area to discuss strengths and needs. If a student is performing below grade level it is imperative for a teacher to backwards assess to identify what grade level or skill a student can complete without support and where they are actually functioning.

If a teacher wants to speak to content standards and grades instead of sub-areas, this is okay the same philosophy applies. If you have a seventh-grade student who is struggling with the section on forces and motion. There is one standard that aligns to this section and it states a student will understand motion, the effects of forces on motion and the graphical representations of motion. This one standard can be broken down into four subsections or objectives. You will need to ask the teacher what concepts were taught to make up this grade and what specific skill with the standard is your child struggling with in this section.

If a teacher can't speak to these areas, it is your job as a parent to push the teacher to know this information. It is also your job as a parent to push teachers to speak to your child's strengths as often as they speak to deficits/needs. This also applies to the child that is above level because in order to grow a student and parent needs to pinpoint areas to work on.

The moral of this section is to ask for specifics and if you don't know what the subareas are ASK! Ask for specifics, ask for written examples, Ask for clarity.

Conversation with teacher/ School

In order to know what your child needs more or less support with, you will need to have a conversation or two with the teachers of each content area. Yes, you need to speak with each teacher for each subject because students perform differently with different teachers and with different subjects. It is typical for schools to have conferences with the homeroom teacher and not the others. You will need to ask questions of this teacher for each subject and if they cannot speak to the specifics ask to conference with each teacher because skill gaps can grow.

You will need to have a conference with teachers at the minimum of each grading period. Most schools don't require this, but you can request this as a parent. Yes, I feel that students need to be involved in conferences at all levels even early elementary. It is one thing for the teacher and parent to know what the student is good at or needs support with, but it is something different for the child to know and to know that you as the parent and teacher are on the same page with providing support.

Also know that students send our progress reports half way through each grading period so you get a halfway check before grades are made official. Also, once students get to about third grade, grades are typically digital and you can request access to view grades through the school grading system platform. This will allow you to check grades more frequently than bi-quarterly.

Intervention

When thinking about interventions think about a school providing your child with the specific support he or she needs. This can be in the form of remediation (below level) or enrichment (above level) and this will tailor instruction to your child. This is the difference between a one size fit all education to tailor made/ specific for me.

Interventions are typically in reading, math and writing but can be in social skills, speech and language, behavior, etc. Reading, writing and math are typically easier for teachers to identify and provide support with because that comes with teaching 101. The later areas are harder to support, not impossible but harder. These require teachers to leave their area(s) of comfort to support your child. This would require them or you to reach out to the counselor, psychologist or speech pathologist for support. Don't let the words I DON'T KNOW stop you or impede your child's success. Ask the question who would know and if this can't be answered ask the assistant principal.

Intervention can be known by other names, but the premise is still the same. Some schools call it response to intervention (RTI), multi-tiered support system (MTSS) or enrichment and intervention (E&I). In essence it consists of three levels or tiers. One tier is whole class instruction, the material that is presented to all students based on their grade level. The second tier is small group intervention, this is the material that is tailored to smaller groups based upon their level in each subject. This is also known as differentiation. The third tier is intensive support and is typically for students that are below grade level and need a higher level of support. With each tier the group of students in them decreases and the frequency that the teacher supports these groups increases.

The material that is given to students are researched based meaning that other schools or states have used this material and there is documentation that it addresses each area being worked on and shows growth. Please don't be naive with the fact that just because this program helps some students and they made gains does not mean that your child will have similar results.

When students are in tier two or three, a teacher will progress monitor each skill to see if students are making growth and if the strategy is beneficial. Progress monitoring is typically done every four to six weeks and intervention/ support should be altered based on the results of the progress monitoring data. Progress monitoring is also standardized; meaning it should be given in the same manner each time and assessment tools need to be uniform from progress monitoring cycle to cycle.

Areas of Eligibility

A student can qualify for special education in one of fourteen areas in the state of North Carolina. This could change from state to state so you can google this information. They are the following: Autism, Deaf-Blindness, Deafness, Developmental Delay, Serious Emotional Disability, Hearing Impairment, Intellectual Disability, Multiple Disabilities, Orthopedic Impairment, Other Health Impairment, Specific Learning Disability, Speech or Language Impairment, Traumatic Brain Injury, and Visual Impairment including blindness. Each of the areas have a worksheet that determines what evaluations and scores students need to obtain to qualify in each specific area.

Once a student has met criteria under one of the fourteen areas, next the student has to meet criteria to receive specially designed instruction. The major question that has to be answered to determine if the student will get an IEP is "Does the impairment negatively impact academics". This is a hard question to answer.

Going into the next step, the initial referral you have to think about and identify what area of eligibility you are going to consider if you decide to evaluate for a disability.

Initial Referral

There are two main ways to have an initial referral. The school can request a meeting once your child has been in the intervention process and has not made expected growth or you can request a meeting based upon your observations and data. The simplest way is from the school because you are going to have to prove and document that a student is performing below grade level expectations and if the child is already in the process this information is readily available. The request from a parent is an avenue but it does not eliminate the intervention step. This part in the process still has to be fulfilled.

At the initial referral meeting, there must be a team of individuals. A team consists of at least a four-person team: the school representative (typically administration), a regular education teacher, the special education teacher and the parent. Once a student can rationalize through thoughts and behaviors, I invite them to the meeting. This isn't required until they are going to turn fourteen during the life of the IEP. As a parent, you can invite them at any time.

The initial referral can be broken down into four parts: identify student strengths, review existing data, reason for the referral, and determination. The first section is to identify the strengths only for your child. During this section you need to look at the whole child so you will look at more than just reading, writing and math. You will also discuss strengths for that area of functional, behavior/ social and communication skills. The second part is to review all data for your child and this needs to encompass at least two years of information because you will need to look for trends. During this part, the team is reviewing attendance, discipline reports, report card grades, local assessments and state assessments, student, parent and teacher input and any outside reports/ evaluations. The third section is to identify the reason for the referral. This is to pinpoint the specific area(s) of need and support. This is when the referral data comes in handy because this information is already identified. If this is a parent referral, this information can be a little tricky to identify but it isn't impossible. You will just have to ask several probing questions to the team members. The fourth part is to make a decision. When making a determination there are three options: determine eligibility with the information you currently have, conduct an evaluation or not conduct an evaluation. With either choice you decide, you have to provide an explanation for the rationale.

If the determination is made not to evaluate the team will complete the summary of documents called the prior written notice and summarize everything that was proposed, determined and rejected during this meeting and document it all.

If your child has been through the intervention process and has a complete file with data and progress monitoring the determination will overwhelmingly be to conduct an evaluation. If the data from the review of records show a negative trend over the last two years (three is ideal) the determination will most likely be to evaluate but the intervention committee will need to start the process immediately. If there are no trends the determination will likely be to not evaluate but a recommendation can be made to the intervention committee to start the intervention process to remediate deficits in noted areas.

In some cases, the parent will bring a completed outside evaluation to the meeting and this data will be reviewed in addition to previous data. A completed outside evaluation has to have educational and psychological assessments. If there is a negative impact on instruction the committee can determine eligibility based on all records presented.

If the team makes the determination to evaluate the student, the team will share with the parent what area or areas of disability that are being considered at this time. Based on the area or areas of disability being considered will determine what assessments will be completed. At this time the team will share a list of assessments and share with the parent. Once this meeting ends and all documents are signed the IEP team will reconvene within 90 days to discuss the results of this meeting. The team will complete the summary called the prior written notice and summarize everything that was proposed, determined and rejected during this meeting and document it all. The team will then sign all documents and the meeting will conclude.

Eligibility

The next meeting that will happen after the initial referral meeting is the eligibility meeting which will discuss the results of all evaluations. I will give three examples of the results that will be discussed. The three categories that are most prevalent in my current school are Specific Learning Disability (SLD), Other Health Impaired (OHI) and Intellectually Disability (ID). The category of Intellectual Disability has three levels: Mild, Moderate and Severe.

All students regardless of the area being considered will have a hearing screening, vision screening, speech screening, observations, social and health history questionnaire, conference with parents, review of educational and behavioral records and progress monitoring in the areas of deficits.

If a student's area of eligibility that was being considered was SLD a student would also have to have educational and psychological assessments completed. If a student's area of eligibility that was being considered was ID a student would have all of the assessments from the SLD in addition to motor screening, health screening, and adaptive behavior assessments. If a student's area of eligibility that was being considered was OHI a student would have the basic requirements of all students being assessed and an educational assessment and medical evaluation.

The results for all screenings and evaluations will be discussed and compared to national norms which mean they will get a level for assessment being below average, average or above average. This can give a comparison to age and grade level peers. During this time, there should be a visual given to you as a parent and it is a standard bell curve. I like to use it to show parents how far their child is performing from average because numbers alone don't mean anything.

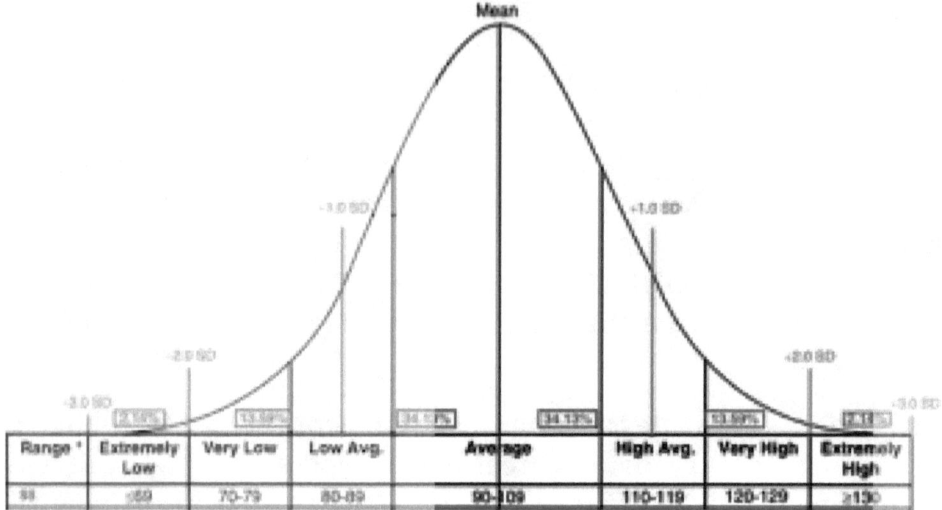

Range	Extremely Low	Very Low	Low Avg.	Average	High Avg.	Very High	Extremely High
ss	≤69	70-79	80-89	90-109	110-119	120-129	≥130

Figure 1

The figure above shows a sample of the bell curve. The numbers can shift based on the assessment and the team can note the change of standard scores (ss).

A student has to meet all criteria of the area of disability. In addition to meeting criteria, there has to be a negative impact on academics to warrant the need for specially designed instruction which will in turn result in creation of an individualized education plan (IEP).

Creation of the IEP

All of the information gathered from the evaluations will guide the creation of the individualized education plan (IEP). The special education teacher will typically draft a version of the IEP based upon the data and present it to the team. At this time the team will go through the entire document and each member will add additional information or reword information to accurately reflect the student's level of need. An IEP will have some components that will not be relevant for all ages and the team will note this. This document is typically uniform for a school, district or state and has to include components for all school ages which are three to twenty-one years old or grades pre-k to 12th.

An IEP is made up of about fourteen sections. Some require little to no involvement on the team's part and other sections are quite detailed. The sections consist of meeting purpose, student profile, assessment summary, source of relevant information, present levels of performance, special factors, goals, services, service goal integration, accommodations, extended school year (ESY), ESY service goal integration, and drafting.

The meeting purpose is the simplest thing to be completed. This is typically done in the introduction, but you state the purpose of the meeting and check to see if there are any questions.

The student profile will take a little more work to complete. You are stating facts that represent the whole child. You will talk about academic and functional skills. You will discuss strengths about the student only. As a parent, you should chime in on the development of this section.

The assessment summary will not be discussed in detail because this section has already been discussed when the evaluation results are shared. The team will note that all items discussed previously will be represented in this section of the IEP.

Based on the subject area(s), that the student qualifies for specially designed instruction the specific tests and subtests will be noted in the source of relevant information section. For example, if the student qualifies for math reasoning and not math calculation. The team will link data points for math reasoning in this section. If the student qualifies under the category of SLD, the team will link all data points from intervention about math reasoning, educational assessment scores for math reasoning and math grades and teacher observations and notes.

The present levels of performance will also be an in-depth section and it will be restating information that has also been previously stated but specific examples will be given, not just standard scores. This section will include strengths and areas of need for the specific area (s). If a student qualifies for more than one area there will be more than one page of present levels of performance. I am going to continue to use the basic reading example. You should be looking for specifics in this area as present levels are discussed.

Example, Carter can read one syllable words with accuracy and independence. He can problem solve words that have phonetic spellings at various levels. He had 100% accuracy with first and second grade words. He knows all short and long vowel sounds in isolation. He is reading with support on a third-grade level at 94% accuracy. He struggles with r-controlled words and patterns. He needs verbal prompting to decode two syllable words in isolation but when reading a text, he can use the text meaning to read 50% of two syllable words. Based on recent intervention data using the Iready benchmark he is working on a second-grade level. Based on the educational assessments conducted, he performed at least 3 years below expectations in basic reading subtests.

The section on special factors is a list of items that you may need to factor into the IEP. You will review if the student has any speech and language concerns, behavior concern, language proficiency concern, adaptive behavior concerns, etc. Some of these concerns may have been noted in the initial referral meeting or these items may have come up through the evaluation process.

Goals will be written in all areas documented in the evaluation system. Goals can be in a plethora of areas. To my knowledge I have written goals in at least 17 areas but there definitely could be more. The areas I have written goals for are: reading fluency, basic reading, reading comprehension, math fluency, math computation, math reasonings, written expression, written composition, vocabulary, self-help, adaptive behavior, listening comprehension, oral expression, self-advocacy, organization, behavior (this is a vast area), and transitions. Goals will need to be specific and measurable. There needs to be clear justification on how the goal will be measured and how often. Example, when given a fifth-grade level writing prompt, Ava will use complete sentence structure when writing a paragraph in 4 out of 5 trials which will be measured by writing samples and informal assessments.

The special education services will give a frequency, duration and location of services. Frequency means how often will specially designed instructions be provided. The frequency can be days a week, days per reporting period or days a school year. The number is typically higher the lower the student's skill level is in each area. Duration means the amount of time for each service. The time can vary in any increment of time and increases based upon skill deficit levels. I have done 5-minute increments for higher level functioning students and for students that need behavior check ins. If the concern is academics, I recommend services be in 15-minute increments because it is easy for students to tell time to the 15 minutes. Location means where the services will be provided. With a typical IEP there are three service locations: regular education classroom, special education classroom or separate school or location. Regular education means this will be in the general education classroom with students with and without disabilities. This is also known as a co-taught setting. The special education classroom means the student will be pulled out and only taught with other students who have disabilities. The separate school or location can be a wide array of locations such as a special education school, hospital, homebound, etc.

Accommodations and modifications are different supports that are put into place to support class instruction, district and state assessments. An accommodation is a support that doesn't alter the material that is being presented to students. Some of the most common accommodations are assistive technology devices, supports for students who are deaf or have extreme hearing loss, dictation to scribe, extended time, read aloud, student marks in book, testing in a separate room, and multiple testing sessions.

A specific example of how an accommodation could be written as follows; In Social Studies, Carter will computerize read aloud features because he has noted reading skills deficits that could impact his ability to read the test. He will be provided with headphones for the read aloud accommodations to ensure that he can head material accurately and to ensure it doesn't distract other testers. Carter will also have the accommodation of testing in a separate room with no more than 10 students to reduce distractions because he has a documented Other Health Impairment that addresses his distractibility on longer assessments. The testing in a separate room accommodation will only be given for assessments and assignments that are longer than 45 minutes.

A modification is a support that alters the complexity of the general education curriculum. When using the ECATS platform, modifications are noted in the other section on the accommodation pages. An example of a modification that you may see on an IEP is as follows: Carter's reading instruction will be provided on his reading level to reduce frustration and to promote independence of tasks based upon his skillset. Carter is currently in 3rd grade and is reading on a level H and he has a 100 Lexile level which is a first grade level, therefore his reading material will be within two levels of his independent reading level if using the letter scale and 100 points if you are using Lexile numbers.

Extended school year (ESY) are services that are provided over the summer and possibly during school intercession for students that have documented skill loss of emerging skills that are vital to their development. If a student is learning to talk, walk or feed themselves and over longer breaks such as fall or winter break, they were noted to lose skills previously mastered they may be determined eligible for these services. Based upon my experience this is mainly for students with lower achievement levels that are in higher grades such as a 4th grader that is just learning to walk or for students with extremely low intellectual quotients (IQs) such as a 45 or less.

The criteria for ESY services change from school district to school district. The determination for eligibility for ESY services will typically require approval from someone higher than the school level because this involves funding. In my current district a district level staff member has to be consulted prior to making the determination to qualify a student for these services.

Service goal integration and ESY service goal integration options are not common with the typical IEP. Service integration is when a related service will link their services with goals that the students already have such as occupational therapy working on basic writing goals. ESY service goals integration is when a student qualifies for supplemental services that are provided over the summer or during school intercessions if they are a year-round school. Both types of integrations are similar in theory because it is an extension of the already existing goals instead of creating a separate set of goals.

The last component is to create the IEP draft and review it for errors because this is the one time that you can see all components in the format that you will print and share with the parent. This is the step that is skipped the most and errors that could be caught are missed. Once the draft is reviewed you create the final copy, sign and print for the parent.

At the end of the meeting a Prior Written Notice (PWN) is completed, signed and printed as well. This document captures the concepts of the meeting that were proposed, rejected and refused. It is similar to the meeting minutes.

Annual Review

An annual review is conducted yearly for each student that has an IEP. Based on the state that you are in will dictate when the meetings are held. Each year they will be held around the same time of the year because an IEP can only span for one calendar year. For example, the IEP's dates will be from 10-11-20 to 10-10-21. The meeting has to happen before the IEP is noted to end. If this doesn't happen this is called a lapse in services. Even if a school continues to provide services the legal document is no longer valid.

As a parent you must have at least 7 business days of notice before the meeting. You can suggest that it is held sooner but the school cannot make this recommendation. As a parent you can decline the meeting date and request a different date based upon your needs. The school staff will inform you if the IEP will lapse if you need to push out the date too far. As a rule of thumb, I ask my teachers to schedule the meeting about a month in advance because many jobs require at least a two week notice before you can be off and accommodating the parent is important.

On the opposite side of the coin, I need you as a parent to know that a meeting can be held without you if proper notice was given and there was no response provided from you as the parent. A school must give two attempts, but I push my teacher to make three contact attempts. The attempts vary in type to help accommodate different parent's response methods. The types that I recommend are as follows: the first attempt is a phone call; the second attempt is the invitation letter be sent home with the student and the third attempt is the invitation letter be mailed home. Many of my teachers have a great text communication and email line with parents so this is okay in place of the letter being sent with the student as long as the parent responds back.

The annual review meeting will go through the entire IEP and make updates based upon new testing and progress monitoring data throughout the year. The data from year to year should not and must not be the same because it is expected that students will grow from year to year even if it is a small amount. For example, the goal from 6th grade may have been to multiply two digits by one digit without regrouping and the goal for 7th grade may be to multiply 2-digit numbers by one-digit numbers with regrouping. If the goal is the same from year to year this should be a red flag for you as a parent. If you are unsure of the goal from the previous year, ask the person leading the meeting to pull it up and show you. Do not just settle for a paraphrase of the goal. Ideally this information would be listed in the present levels of performance. For example, Carter's math calculation goal previously was to solve math problems that multiplied two-digit numbers by one-digit numbers, and he mastered this goal with 80% accuracy.

Addendum

Addendums are meetings that happen if a correction needs to be made or to correct errors that are found in IEPs after you review it. My rule of thumb is to always have an IEP meeting with the team but there are some instances that a school district may say you don't have to have a formal meeting just notify the parent and make the correction.

There are several reasons that I have had to conduct an addendum. First, there is an assessment that I forgot to click, and the student is taking this assessment this year and needs modifications or accommodations based upon a similar test. The student could have the 7th grade Science North Carolina Final Exam (NCFE) but in 8th grade they take an End of Grade (EOG) assessment, these are two separate tests and they both need to be on the 7th grade IEP. Second, I have forgotten to click a button on a page that makes the determination for Extended School Year (ESY) and this information was not discussed therefore a meeting has to happen to fix this error. Third I have had to correct IEP dates because it has different service areas ending at separate times and this was not discussed and decided upon in the IEP meeting based on the Prior Written Notice (PWN).

Addendums are the avenue to correct human errors. Even with a team of four people in a meeting accident happen and they have to legally be corrected.

Manifestation Determination Review (MDR)

Once a student with an IEP or in the evaluation process to be considered for an (IEP) has been suspended for 10 school days a meeting must take place to determine if the incident is related to the suspected disability. This meeting is called a manifestation determination review which will determine if the disability manifested to cause the incident that caused the suspension.

Each state and school district have different rules about how this meeting is supposed to be conducted but I am going to discuss the basic concepts regarding this type of meeting. For the district that I currently work in the meeting time frame is different. The meeting is supposed to happen within three days after the 10th suspension. The meeting invitation will look different from a typical invitation because the incident and number of days suspended should be on the invitation. The invitation should be sent home the same day the student is suspended. This can be tricky because if the student gets suspended at the end of the day and the special education teacher isn't available then the invitation can't go home. I gave the administrators at my school a short script to say to parents if this is the case and the administrators will schedule the meeting at this time as well.

Sample Script wording for special education teacher or administrators

Mr. or Mrs. Mapp your son/ daughter has been suspended for __ days for violating school code ___. You child has an IEP therefore we have to schedule an MDR meeting in the next three days. Which day __ or __ work best for you at 2:30pm. Would you like me to send a copy of the invitation in the mail or do you want me to email it to you?

This meeting has three major components. The first component consists of reviewing the current disciplinary action. With this component, you will review the data that was provided to the team to include but not limited to the referral, offender's statement, witness' statement(s). The second component is the review of data used. There will be a review of records with an emphasis on behavior. The team will look at the most recent evaluations, IEP progress, accommodations and modifications and any other pertinent information that team members have to share. The third section is the assessment of the manifestation which consists of 4 questions to answer about the disability and the incident to determine if there is a correlation/ link between the two.

If the team determines that the incident is a manifestation of the disability the suspension days will be removed from the system and the student will be allowed to return to school. If the incident is not determined to be a manifestation of the student's disability the student will remain out of school for the remainder of the suspension time.

There will be a manifestation determination review meeting after every suspension once the student reaches 10 days. If you have one review meeting you will continue having them for the remainder of the school year if the student is suspended again. Each school year the student starts with a clean slate.

Reevaluations

A reevaluation meeting takes place every three years; some districts call them triennial evaluations. Reevaluations are when the team meets to see if the student needs another set of assessments which can be similar to the initial evaluation. The team has three options to think about at each reevaluation meeting. The team can decide to conduct a comprehensive evaluation which would be identical to the initial evaluation, the team can also determine that only a few assessments need to be reevaluated. The IEP team can determine that the previous assessments are deemed relevant and not conduct any new assessments.

If the team determines that there needs to be assessments conducted the reevaluation meeting will have two parts. During the first meeting the team will determine that additional testing is needed, and the team will get consent from the parent to conduct the evaluations. The second meeting would be to discuss the evaluation results and revise the IEP. This is similar to the initial referral.

During the initial meeting, if the team decides that no additional assessments are needed the team will redetermine eligibility using previous assessment data and revise the IEP based upon all information reviewed.

Note to remember. The IEP should be reviewed after every re-evaluation meeting.

Related Services

Related Services are services that students are determined eligible for based on the initial evaluation or reevaluation. The most common related services are: Speech & Language, Counseling, Occupational Therapy, Physical Therapy, Interpreters and Audiology. There is a set of eligibility criteria for each of the related services. If the student is new to the school or new concerns arise all these related services are indirectly observed by one or more of the assessors/ evaluators conducting assessments. With the typical evaluation, speech and language skills are assessed, hearing is assessed to determine if audiology needs to be involved, observations are conducted to determine if counseling needs to be assessed and during each assessment evaluators review motor skills unofficially to determine if occupational or physical therapy needs to be assessed. A sign language interpreter are needed based upon known needs such as a student being deaf or hard of hearing.

Based on the notes and observations of the evaluators, if a concern is noted the team will reconvene to add additional assessments for the specific areas of concern. The meeting will consist of repeating the initial evaluation meeting components and adding areas of concern and getting consent from the parent to assess this area.

Related services can have their own separate goals and service time, or they can be integrated into other goals that the student already has if this is a reevaluation.

Currently in the state that I work, the only related service that can stand alone and have its own IEP is the area of Speech and Language. Other areas can be serviced through other school related support programs.

Transition Services

Think of transition services as any time your child has a major move or shift in services. The major transitions that your child will have are: early services (before age 3) to public schools (third birthday), elementary to middle school, middle school to high school and high school to independent living. There will be a separate meeting outside of the yearly meeting.

During these shifts' services can change but they don't have to; so, focus and ask questions during these meetings. Don't allow services and accommodations to be altered or removed just because there is a change.

I also ask that you don't remain closed minded to change. For example, a big change that can happen from elementary to middle school is the notion of inclusion and learning lab. If your child attends a school that only offers special education services in a special setting this could be to your child's disservices depending upon their level of functioning and academic levels. If you are expecting your child to be independent and attend college, you need to think about inclusive services because your child will need to work on grade level content in a larger setting.

Final Thoughts

The world of special education is complicated in many aspects and I look at it from the lens of a mom, educator, advocate and school leader. No two cases are identical, but strategies can work for multiple kids once you figure out trends and patterns in behaviors and gaps. It is a world of doing your homework or asking people you know and trust for help. As a teacher starting out, I couldn't do it alone and I was "trained" and as an advocate and school leader I am constantly rethinking things I thought I knew and thought was right. Students daily push me to rethink concepts and my current practices and parents/guardians push me to see their kid in every one of my decisions.

As a parent I would URGE you to do your homework and learn from past lessons and meetings. You are the expert on your child, and you have a voice in every meeting. I would always ask for all decisions to be data driven and ask to see the data. The water can easily be muddied if feelings get involved. Keep a notebook or folder with all information on your child. Ask for copies of data for your files. If you are new to special education or a new school, ask for a draft copy of all meeting documents before the meeting so you can review them. Lots of information is thrown out in meetings and if your processing of information isn't quick you need to review it so you can ask proper questions in the meeting. Also ask your child about what they like and don't like about school and classes especially the area(s) that they receive support.

Questions to ask in meetings:
1. Show me the data for this goal/decision.
2. Is this action/behavior happening in all classes?
3. Which teachers provided input on this topic?
4. What other strategies have/can you use?

Acknowledgements

Thanks to my awesome husband who allows and pushes me to do everything that I put my mind, heart and energy into. Thanks to my kids for pushing me to work fast at all times because they will only allow short bursts of alone time. Thanks to my online professional learning network who put timelines and ideas in my mind to help build a legacy for my family. Thank you to the Holy Spirit who allowed the words to flow when I didn't know what to write.

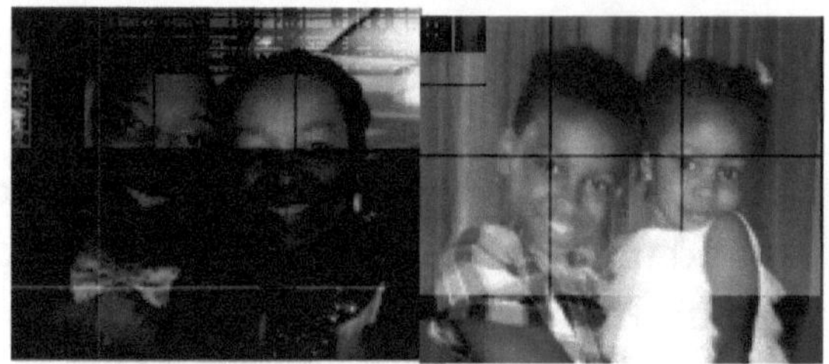

About the Author

I am a Woman of God that lives by the scripture 1 Thessalonians 5:16-18.

I am a Wife to a wonderful husband & dad; Love you Anthony (smiles), Dion!

I am a Mom with two awesome, extremely different kids, Carter & Ava.

I am an Educator with 16 years of experience in grade pre-k- 8th grade. #Lexington2SC #UnionCountyNC #CharMeckCountyNC

I am an Advocate that wants to know better in order to do better.

I am Dr. Sophia Latrell Davis Crawford Mapp! There is a story and educational journey behind all 6 of those names that define who I am.

I started school at 3 years old and completed the journey at 36 with a Doctorate! #MarionCountySchoolsSC #PresbyterianCollege #ColumbiaCollege #WingateUniversity #ConverseCollege #GardnerWebbUniversity